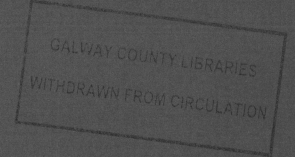

STAR  FILES

Jackie Chan

Dan Fox

Raintree

www.raintreepublishers.co.uk
Visit our website to find out more information about **Raintree** books.

To order:
☎ Phone 44 (0) 1865 888113
🖷 Send a fax to 44 (0) 1865 314091
💻 Visit the Raintree Bookshop at **www.raintreepublishers.co.uk** to browse our catalogue and order online.

GALWAY COUNTY LIBRARIES

J2033 €50

€19·25

Produced for Raintree by
White-Thomson Publishing Ltd
Bridgewater Business Centre
210 High Street, Lewes, BN7 2NH

First published in Great Britain by Raintree,
Halley Court, Jordan Hill, Oxford OX2 8EJ,
part of Harcourt Education.
Raintree is a registered trademark of
Harcourt Education Ltd.

© Harcourt Education Ltd 2005
The moral right of the proprietor has
been asserted.

Editorial: Catherine Clarke, Sarah Shannon and
Kate Buckingham
Design: Leishman Design and Michelle Lisseter
Picture Research: Catherine Clarke
Production: Chloe Bloom

Originated by Modern Age
Printed and bound in China by South China
Printing Company

ISBN 1 844 43295 5
09 08 07 06 05
10 9 8 7 6 5 4 3 2 1

**British Library Cataloguing in
Publication Data**
Fox, Dan
Jackie Chan. – (Star Files)
791.4'3'028'092
A full catalogue record for this book is
available from the British Library.

Acknowledgements
The publishers would like to thank the
following for permission to reproduce
photographs: Allstar Cinetext Collection pp. **16**,
19 (t), **23**, **25**, **26** (b), **27**, **30** (t), **30** (b), **33** (t),
36 (b), **37**; Allstar Collection pp. **13** (b), **15** (t),
29 (b), **40**; Allstarpl.com pp. **21** (t). **24**, **36** (t);
Corbis pp. **4** (Reuters), **6**, **12** (Reuters), **15** (b)
(Neal Preston), **17** (b) (Images.com), **17** (t)
(Reuters/Jan Pitman/Pool), **18** (Buena Vista
Pictures/David Appleby), **19** (b) (SYGMA/Sunset
Boulevard), **20** (SYGMA), **21** (b) (Reuters), **22**
(Bettmann), **26** (t), **28** (Neal Preston), **29** (t), **31**
(Reuters/Kin Cheung), **32** (Reuters), **33** (b)
(SYGMA/Frank Trapper), **34** (SYGMA/Frank
Trapper), **38** (b) (Mitchell Gerber), **39**
(Reuters/China Photos), **41** (Reuters), **42**
(Reuters/Grigoris Siamidis), **43** (t) (SYGMA/Rick
Maiman); Getty Images (Photodisc) pp. **10**, **13**
(t), **35** (t), **43** (b); iStockPhoto pp. **9**, **14**;
Powerstock (ImageSource) p. **7** (t); Retna UK
p. **7** (b) (Craig Barritt); Rex Features pp. **5**
(Stewart Cook), **8** (Sipa Press), **11** (Crollalanza),
35 (b) (Peter Brooker), **38** (t) (Peter Brooker).
Cover image reproduced with permission of Rex
Features (Stewart Cook).

Quote sources: p. **9** Jackie Chan, interview with
Dr Craig D. Read, *Bright Lights Film Journal*, issue
13, 1994; p. **13** Jackie Chan, *I am Jackie Chan*;
p. **14** Master Yu Jim-yuen, *I am Jackie Chan*;
p. **16** Jackie Chan, *I am Jackie Chan*; p. **21** Jackie
Chan, interview with Ian Rogers, for *FilmZone*,
19/12/1994; p. **22** Jackie Chan, *Hong Kong Film
Connection*, Volume III, issue 5, 1996; p. **24**
Jackie Chan, *Entertainment Weekly*, 16/2/1996
p. **26** Jackie Chan, *I am Jackie Chan*; p. **28** Jackie
Chan, *Hello* magazine, www.hellomagazine.com
/profiles, 2004; p. **32** Jackie Chan, *I am Jackie
Chan*; p. **41** Jackie Chan, *I am Jackie Chan*; p. **42**
Jackie Chan, UN news conference, Cambodia,
quoted on www.bbc.co.uk 26/4/2004.

The publishers would like to thank Rosie Nixon,
Charly Rimsa, Sarah Williams, Marie Lorimer
and Nicola Hodgson for their assistance in the
preparation of this book.

Contents

Any words appearing in the text in bold, **like this**, are explained in the glossary. You can also look out for them in the Star words box at the bottom of each page.

Action hero

Mixing comedy and action is very hard to do. Jackie Chan has made his name doing just that. He is famous for using **martial arts** and dramatic stunts in his incredible films.

Born to perform

Jackie wanted to be a star from the age of seven. His parents sent him to a school with a very tough master where he learnt how to be a performer.

ALL ABOUT JACKIE

Full name: Jackie Chan
Other names: Chan Kong-sang, Yuen Lo, Sing Lung
Born: 7 April 1954
Place of birth: Hong Kong
Height: 5 feet 8 inches (1.72 metres)
Family: Father: Charles Chan, Mother: Lee-lee Chan, Wife: Lin Feng-jiao, Son: (Jackson Chan Cho-Ming – known as Jaycee) born in 1983, Daughter: from relationship with Elaine Ng Yi-Lei (Etta Ng Chok Lam) born in 1998
Big breaks: *Drunken Master*, his first smash hit film in Hong Kong, and *Rumble in the Bronx* in Hollywood
Other interests: Singing, charity work

Jackie is famous around the world for his martial arts skill.

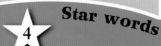
Star words martial arts type of fighting based on self-defence and single combat

Jackie has become famous for mixing action with fun!

Find out later

Who helped make Jackie's film style popular in Hollywood?

How many music albums has Jackie made?

Where does Jackie live when he is in Hollywood?

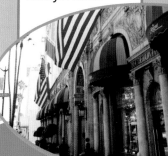

Fighting fit

Jackie combines gymnastics, **kung fu**, and **daredevil** action in his films. He has worked very hard to earn his **reputation**. Unlike many action stars, he does nearly all his own stunts.

East to West

Across the world, people love watching Jackie Chan films. When he started out in Hong Kong, he was not able to make the kind of films he liked. Once he showed that action films could be funny, he became famous. Now he is known wherever he goes.

reputation being well-known for something

Early life

Ever since he was born, Jackie has been different. Most babies are born after 9 months, but Jackie took 12 months! He was a very big baby and his mum had to have an operation to help her give birth to him. He weighed 5.4 kilograms (12 pounds).

Jackie was born in Hong Kong.

Chinese years

In the Chinese calendar, each year is named after one of twelve animals. They all have different meanings. The year Jackie was born – 1954 – was the year of the horse. This is a sign of hard work, energy, and good fortune.

⭐ Star fact

Jackie had a different name when he was born. His parents called him Chan Kong-sang, which means "Born in Hong Kong" Chan. Jackie's mum nicknamed him "Pao-pao" (cannonball) because he was so big and heavy.

Not for sale

The hospital bill for the operation was US$26. Jackie's parents were very poor and could not afford to pay. The **surgeon** offered to adopt Jackie and pay the medical bills. Jackie's parents did not want to give him up. They knew there was something special about their only son. Charles Chan borrowed the money from his friends to pay the bill.

Star words

ambassador someone who works for their country, inside a foreign country

Housekeepers

Jackie's parents lived and worked at the French **Embassy** in Hong Kong. His dad was the cook and his mum was the housekeeper. She did all the washing for the **ambassador** and his family. The house was a mansion, but Jackie's family only had a small room at the back to live in. It had no windows and hardly any furniture. It measured about four long steps from one wall to the other.

Life on the Peak

The French Embassy was in a rich area called Victoria Peak, although Jackie and his family were not wealthy. They worked hard and felt lucky to be in such a nice house.

Thrown out

When Jackie was naughty, his dad locked him away with the rubbish bins. He had to sleep there all night. Luckily, his mum was a bit kinder. She would sneak food to him over the top of the door.

Jackie always seems to have a smile on his face! As a child, things were not so happy for him.

embassy home and offices of an ambassador in a foreign country
surgeon special doctor who does operations

Early exercise

Every morning, Jackie's dad woke him up before the sun rose. He took him to a room in the house that he had made into a gym, using rope and bags filled with sand. They would run, do press-ups, and lift weights.

★ ★ ★ ★ ★ ★ ★ ★ ★ ★

Hospital help

Jackie knows that he is **fortunate**, and likes to help others. When he first became famous, he was asked to give out some presents to children in hospital. Seeing how happy they were, Jackie took his own presents the year after.

★ ★ ★ ★ ★ ★ ★ ★ ★ ★

⭐ Star fact

Jackie does Northern style kung fu, which uses spinning kicks more than punches.

Jackie trained hard to learn kung fu.

Learning kung fu

After they had exercised, they practised **kung fu** fighting. Jackie's dad came from a warrior family in a place called Shandong in China. **Discipline** and hard work were important to him and he taught Jackie how to fight with honour and respect. These early-morning training sessions were the beginning of Jackie's **martial arts** skills.

Jackie loves food and a full belly!

Learning a lesson

Jackie went to his first school aged six. It was called Nan Hua Elementary **Academy** and was at the bottom of Victoria Peak. He hated it straightaway and got bad marks.

66 Don't practise kung fu just to be like Jackie Chan... stay in school, study hard... 99

A long walk

Jackie used to spend his money for the bus home on food. Then he would walk back up the hill. The other boys in the area were rich and teased him for being poor. Jackie often got into fights with them.

Changing school

Jackie's dad got a job in the American **Embassy** in Australia. Jackie was sent to a boarding school in Hong Kong called the China Drama Academy. He was there for 10 years!

Food, glorious food!

One of Jackie's favourite things is food. When he was a child there was sometimes hardly anything to eat. The family usually ate meat or fried fish with rice and pickled vegetables. Jackie says there is nothing as important as a full belly!

fortunate lucky

School rules

A school day

Each day the pupils woke up at 5 a.m. They did gymnastics and **martial arts** for 5 hours. After lunch, they did **flexibility** exercises until dinner and then had classroom lessons. There were more exercises until bedtime at midnight – even at weekends!

★ ★ ★ ★ ★ ★ ★ ★ ★ ★

At first, Jackie thought the China Drama **Academy** was perfect. He was allowed to practice **kung fu** all day, with hardly any normal lessons. However, it soon became tough.

Learning the hard way

The teacher in charge was called Master Yu Jim-Yuen and he believed in strong **discipline**. Each day, he made Jackie and all the other children do difficult exercises. They had to do handstands for half an hour at a time, and were punished if they moved a muscle!

Tough training

Master Yu was like a father to the pupils, but he was very strict. Jackie did not like him then, but now he realizes that Master Yu helped to make him famous.

Other pupils

The boys and girls at the academy called each other brothers and sisters. At night, they slept on the floor of the big practice hall, with only a blanket to keep them warm.

Jackie learned to be a gymnast, which made him flexible.

Star words   flexibility bending and stretching

Big Brothers

The eldest boy was called "Biggest Brother". He made the younger children do what he wanted. Yuen Lung was Biggest Brother for most of Jackie's time there. He was one of the biggest and best fighters, and he bullied Jackie.

Stage set

The pupils were at the academy to learn how to perform Chinese opera. Jackie saw his first Chinese opera at the Lai Yuen amusement park and immediately wanted to be on the stage.

 **Star fact**

Jackie's name when he arrived at the academy was still Chan Kong-sang. Master Yu renamed him "Yuen Lo".

★ ★ ★ ★ ★ ★ ★ ★ ★ ★

Chinese opera

Chinese opera is different from Western opera. As well as singing and acting, there is gymnastics, combat, and **mime**. The actors all wear amazing costumes and it is very dramatic to watch!

★ ★ ★ ★ ★ ★ ★ ★ ★ ★

Jackie hated Yuen Lung at the academy. Now he is called Samo Hung and they are good friends.

Making films

The first film that Jackie ever appeared in was called *Big and Little Wong Tin-Bar*. He was 8 years old. Li Li-hua, a famous Taiwanese actress, played his mum. She asked for Jackie to play her son in other films, too.

★ ★ ★ ★ ★ ★ ★ ★ ★ ★

Lucky seven

Jackie had to wait a while before he got on stage for the first time. Then, one day, Master Yu chose the seven best performers at the **academy** to act in an opera called *The Seven Little Fortunes*. It was a big honour for Jackie to be selected. The group became known as the Seven Little Fortunes from then on.

A natural actor

Jackie loved being in the spotlight. His big chance came to play the lead role in an opera. He enjoyed the roar of the crowd as he acted and sang. This was his first taste of the audience cheering for him – and Jackie wanted more!

Jackie still loves cheering crowds – and he has plenty of fans!

Star words   performance acting out a show

Fame and fortune

The Seven Little Fortunes performed many more operas. Most of them took place at the Lai Yuen amusement park, where Jackie had first watched opera.

The dream. Applause, the cheering of the crowd, fame and glory. It was about to come true!

Stage dive

In one **performance**, Jackie's mask slipped down so he could not see what he was doing. He fell right off the stage!

Girl trouble

Jackie met his first girlfriend when he was performing opera for the academy. Her name was Oh Chang and she was performing for another school. The day after the show, he asked her out. He saw her every day for nearly a year, but they were forced to split up because her father did not like Jackie.

Bread bin

After one show, the Seven Little Fortunes were hungry. The food stalls were closed, but Jackie sneaked into one and took some stale crusts from the bin. Master Yu caught them and they were punished!

Jackie has got used to diving around during filming on his movies!

Starting stunts

As he got older, Jackie was hired as a **stuntman** for Hong Kong films. He was a popular choice because he was well-trained, **flexible**, and good at gymnastics. This meant he could do difficult stunts without getting badly hurt. He was also very brave and often did risky stunts that others did not want to try.

Jackie must have been fearless to jump from the top of a Hong Kong bus.

Career choice

Jackie still went to the **academy** when he was not working, but he enjoyed getting to meet other stuntmen and famous actors. Jackie knew that this was what he wanted to do for a living. He started to dream of becoming a star.

Lucky landing

The first big jump that Jackie remembers doing was from a Hong Kong bus as a young boy. When the conductor caught him without a ticket, he leapt head first out of an upstairs window and landed in a bush by the roadside.

Leaving school

All of the Seven Little Fortunes were growing up. Biggest Brother changed his name to Samo Hung and left the academy to become a **professional** stuntman.

Jackie was 17 years old and thought it was time to leave the academy himself. Chinese opera was no longer popular, so he decided to become a professional stuntman and actor.

> 66 You're grown men now. You've grown wings. You can fly. (Master Yu) 99

Star words   professional being paid to do something as a job

Aches and pains

Being a stuntman on the Hong Kong film scene was difficult and dangerous. They did not get paid very much money. One of the other stuntmen told Jackie, "We get paid in scars and bruises."

Stuntmen usually get to do the things that no one else wants to!

Samo Hung played one of the lead characters in a popular television series called *Martial Law*.

Leading the way

Soon, Jackie got a **reputation** as the best stuntman around. He did not get a lead acting role until a film called *The Little Tiger of Canton* in 1971. Unfortunately, it was made very cheaply and was not good enough to make him a star.

stuntman person who stands in for an actor during dangerous scenes

A dragon is born

Bruce Lee

Bruce Lee was a brilliant fighter, who made martial arts films more exciting than anyone before him. His nickname was "little dragon". In 1973 Bruce Lee died **tragically** of a **brain oedema**, aged 32. Over 27,000 people attended his memorial services.

A new film company called Golden Harvest started up in Hong Kong. They had a young star working for them called Bruce Lee. He made **martial arts** films very popular with his film *The Big Boss* in 1971.

Getting noticed

Samo Hung worked for Golden Harvest. He got Jackie a stunt job on Bruce Lee's next film, *Fist of Fury*. As well as doing some minor stunts, Jackie was the **body double** for the **villain**, Mr Suzuki.

Lee kicked Jackie out of a door. With the help of some wires, he flew 6 metres (20 feet) through the air, the furthest distance ever by a Hong Kong **stuntman**. Jackie landed on concrete and was knocked out!

Bruce Lee has become a martial arts **icon** and his films are still very popular today.

❝ I think that audiences want to see someone who's just a man. Like them. Who has a sense of humour. ❞

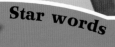

Star words

body double person who looks like an actor in a film and replaces them in some scenes

G'day Jackie

After Bruce Lee died, **kung fu** films became less popular. Jackie worked on a film called *Hand of Death*, but he could not get any work afterwards. He went to stay with his parents in Australia.

He worked on a building site, with his dad's friend Jack. The other builders could not say his name (Kong-Sang), so they called him Jack, too. After a while, it became Jackie, which has stuck ever since.

The new dragon

Jackie went back to Hong Kong, where a director called Lo Wei wanted him to be the new Bruce Lee. He gave him the nickname "Sing Lung". In China, he is still known as this today.

Jackie is an expert at making funny faces to show pain in his films.

Jackie was renamed Sing Lung, which means "already a dragon".

Acting strange

Jackie did not like the tough and serious style that Bruce Lee used. He wanted to be himself. So, he developed his own way of doing things – making fighting look funny, but still very skillful. Jackie's action comedy style was born!

brain oedema swelling of the brain
tragic very sad

17

Making films

Jackie's first film back in Hong Kong was *New Fist of Fury*, in 1976. It was a **flop** at the **box office** because the director, Lo Wei, made him act like Bruce Lee, instead of how he wanted to. The same happened with his next film that year, *Shaolin Wooden Men*.

Meeting Willie

One good thing that came from making these films was working with Willie Chan. He was general manager of Lo Wei's film company. Willie told Lo Wei that Jackie should be allowed to act how he wanted.

Using his loaf

With more freedom, Jackie made the comedy *Half a Loaf of* **Kung Fu**. Lo Wei hated it and locked it away in a safe.

Bright and cheerful

Willie Chan is a colourful character. He has helped make Jackie the superstar he is today. Willie is famous for his very bright clothes. He is not related to Jackie, but they are very good friends.

⭐ Star fact

In his films, Jackie often beats up people twice his size, and fights entire crowds at once. Jackie says: "I don't think I'd enjoy seeing if I could do the same in real life."

Star words

box office place where tickets are sold. If a film does well at the box office it means that lots of people paid to go and see it.

Many years after the original *Drunken Master* film, Jackie also starred in the sequel.

Like Robin Hood!

Wong Fei-Hong was like a Chinese Robin Hood. He helped weak and sick people. He was a powerful martial artist, who used a "drunken" fighting style as his secret weapon. Like Robin Hood (below) his story has often been told in films.

Snake success

Jackie was forced by Lo Wei to make more films he did not like. In 1978, he was **loaned** to a new film company called Seasonal. The first film he starred in for them was *Snake in Eagle's Shadow*. It had the fast action of a kung fu film, but because it was also a comedy, it was different from anything before it. The film became the biggest smash hit in Hong Kong history.

Funny fighting

Jackie made his next film, *Drunken Master*, with the same company. The story was based on the Chinese hero Wong Fei-Hong. Jackie fought with a funny, clumsy style. This film was an even bigger success than *Snake in Eagle's Shadow*!

flop film that people do not like, and that does not make any money

19

Stuntman

Becoming the best

Jackie is a **perfectionist**. If a stunt does not work properly, he does it again. In his early career, the other Hong Kong **stuntmen** called him "Double Boy" because he would do two takes to make sure it looked right.

★ ★ ★ ★ ★ ★ ★ ★ ★ ★

It is not surprising that Jackie has broken many bones!

Although Jackie created his own style of action comedy, he has become most famous for his stunts. A lot of top actors use a stunt double for dangerous scenes in their films. Jackie is proud that he has always done most of his own stunts. This makes his films look more **realistic** and exciting.

Star fact

Jackie holds the Guinness world record for the most stunts by a living actor.

Giving it everything

In Hong Kong, before he became famous, Jackie learnt how to be "lung fu mo shi". This means "dragon tiger" – brave, strong, and powerful. He acts this way in all his stunts. In each film, the stunts are bigger and better than in the last one. This also makes them more risky, and Jackie has been hurt many times.

Star words

perfectionist someone who tries hard to get things right
realistic like real life

Laughing at danger

A lot of Jackie's **slapstick** style came from watching old silent films. The stars of these films had to use action because there was no talking.

One of his favourite silent film actors is Buster Keaton. Like Jackie, he always wanted his stunts to be real for the audience. By doing very daring feats with a silly grin or a confused face, Keaton made them look funny.

> **"**I want to be remembered like I remember Buster Keaton.**"**

A comic great

Buster Keaton (above) was born in 1895. He was on stage from when he was a baby, then learned how to use a camera to make funny films. He was very talented, but, like Jackie, he got injured a lot.

Fun and fear

Jackie enjoys making difficult things seem simple, too. He shows the pain when it hurts, but always comes out smiling. This is how Jackie mixes comedy and action. He gives a "thumbs up" when he completes a really dangerous stunt.

Injury list

Some of Jackie's injuries:
- punctured skull
- crushed legs
- broken nose
- dislocated cheek, sternum (chest), shoulder, and pelvis
- broken ankle

Jackie's trademark "thumbs up".

slapstick using actions to be funny, instead of words

One and only

Jackie is the master of the "super-stunt". He is not happy just doing what has been done before. He always wants to push himself and do almost impossible feats. By being different, he is truly **unique**.

By this time, Jackie had worked as an actor and stuntman in lots of films.

Super-stunts

All of Jackie's training as a **stuntman** made him more and more **creative** in each film. By the time he made *Project A*, in 1983, he was ready to do stunts that were more dangerous than ever.

In his first "**super-stunt**", Jackie jumped from a tower on to a clock hand, 15 metres (50 feet) above the ground. Then he let go, with only two cloth canopies to break his fall.

I don't do special effects. It's not like Superman.

Jumping Jackie

It took Jackie a week to build up the courage to do the stunt. When he did, he landed on his neck, but was not happy with the way it looked on film. So he got up and did it twice more!

Star words

choreograph   plan the moves carefully, like a dance
creative   showing imagination

The same year he made *Police Story*, Jackie played the role of a New York cop in *The Protector*.

Pain barrier

Even though he always does spectacular stunts, Jackie still knows the meaning of fear. Lots of people have called him crazy for doing such dangerous things on film. He has hurt himself many times, often quite badly.

Danger man

It is because he wants his films to be the best that Jackie is willing to take big risks. He knows that no one else will dare to do what he does, so his films will always look more amazing. He **choreographs** all of his fights, to make sure they are exciting on film. He will often take days to shoot one scene, to get it looking just right.

A big shock!

Jackie's biggest stunt in the film *Police Story* was a three-storey slide down a pole wrapped in lights. The electrician was supposed to plug them into a small battery. But he used a wall socket instead and Jackie burnt the skin on his hands!

super-stunt very difficult and dangerous stunt
unique only one

No insurance!

There is a lot of danger involved with doing the stunts that Jackie is famous for. Even simple stunts can be risky. He cannot get **insurance** for his films. If anyone gets hurt on his film set, he pays for all the medical bills himself!

★ ★ ★ ★ ★ ★ ★ ★ ★ ★

Cheating death

The stunt that came closest to killing Jackie was not a very difficult one, by Jackie's standards. It happened during the filming of *Armour of God*, when he fell from a tree branch that could not hold his weight.

> "I get hurt, but the movie gets released for 100 years. It's OK that I broke my leg for three months!"

Brain basher

He landed head first on a rock from 4.5 metres (15 feet) above the ground. Blood squirted out of his ears because he hit his head so hard. Jackie had to be rushed to hospital.

A brain **surgeon** took out a piece of broken bone in his head. A plastic plug was put in to seal up the hole. It is still there now. Jackie also lost some hearing in one ear.

With no insurance, Jackie's leaps on screen can be expensive!

Star words   insurance money paid out in case of an accident or injury

Stunts

Jackie's favourite stunts:

1. Police Story village car chase
2. Police Story pole slide
3. Project A clock tower fall
4. Police Story 3 helicopter jump
5. Who Am I? Slide down building

Jackie's jump in *Police Story 3*.

Flying leap

Although all his stunts are dangerous, Jackie went to extremes in his 1992 film, *Police Story 3*. He leapt from the top of a building to grab on to a rope ladder hanging from a helicopter. There was no safety net, so he had to get it right first time!

Slippery slope

In *Who Am I?* Jackie fights on the rooftop of a building, 21 storeys up. He ends up sliding down the sloped side of the building – all the way to the ground. It was so dangerous it was 2 weeks before he was ready to do it.

Jackie's combination of stunts with **kung fu** action is what makes his films so exciting.

The Sing Ga Ban

Jackie's co-stars have to be good **stuntmen**, too. He set up the Sing Ga Ban (Jackie Chan Stuntman Association). They are a team who appear in all of Jackie's films to make the action look right.

Making it big

Jackie's next aim was Hollywood.

After Jackie's success in Hong Kong, he had become well-known there. He was still young and had appeared in lots of films. People recognized him in the street and looked forward to his films. In 1979, he had another hit with his first attempt at directing, *Fearless Hyena*. He also starred in the huge success, *The Young Master*.

> "Hollywood, I thought to myself, ready or not, here I come!"

Pop hit

Jackie had to learn to roller skate for *The Big Brawl*. He was skating by the beach in California, when he literally bumped into Teresa Teng Li-jun, one of China's most famous popstars! For a while, they became a celebrity couple.

Go west

Jackie was not yet famous outside of Asia. His next step was to try to make it in Hollywood. He went to the United States to film *The Big Brawl*. There was a good cast, but it did not do well. US film companies did not let Jackie use his Hong Kong stunt style.

Jackie in the 1980 film *The Big Brawl*.

Star words

out-takes scenes that were not used in a film because they went wrong

Jackie in *Cannonball Run 2* with Burt Reynolds, the star of the film.

American dream

Jackie's next film in the United States was the 1981 film *The Cannonball Run*, with lots of world-famous stars. Even though he only had a small part, it was Jackie's big chance to show what he could do.

Big flop

The film itself was a success, but it was no good for Jackie's career. His English was bad and his character did not show off his skills in the best way. His fans in Asia did not like it either. Worst of all, he was forced to film *Cannonball Run 2* because it was in his contract.

Heading home

Jackie was fed up with being told what to do. So he went back to Hong Kong to make Jackie-style films again.

The best bits

The Cannonball Run showed **out-takes** as the credits rolled at the end of the film. Jackie has used this idea ever since. You can see some of the most funny or painful out-takes from Jackie's films at the end!

Together again

Jackie had more hits in Asia with *Project A* and *Wheels on Meals*. He filmed them both with two of his friends from the China Drama **Academy**, Samo Hung and Yuen Biao. They worked very well together because they had all been through the same hard training.

" My life is the movies. "

Superstition

Wheels on Meals was filmed in Spain. The name was changed from "Meals on Wheels" because too many films that began with "m" had **flopped**!

Playing around

Jackie and his *Wheels on Meals* co-star Benny "The Jet" Urquidez teased each other about which of them would win in a real fight. Urquidez is one of the best foreign fighters Jackie has worked with.

Benny "The Jet" Urquidez.

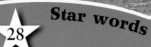

Out of luck

More success followed in Asia with *My Lucky Stars*. After proving he was still popular, Jackie tried to make it in the West again in *The Protector*. Jackie did not agree with the director on how it should be filmed. It was a disaster at the **box office** and the chance to be big in the United States was gone again. He left once more, disappointed.

Hong Kong hits

One director that Jackie has always **admired** is Steven Spielberg. In the 1986 film, *Armour of God*, Jackie played a character called Asian Hawk. This character was based on Indiana Jones – the hero of Spielberg's *Raiders of the Lost Ark*. *Armour of God* became another massive hit for Jackie, along with the action classic, *Police Story*.

Breaking records

Jackie's 1985 film *My Lucky Stars* made 30 million Hong Kong dollars for the film company, Golden Harvest. They paid for an ice sculpture in the shape of a 30 million Hong Kong dollar sign – which Jackie and the other members of the crew smashed!

Jackie's character in *Armour of God* was based on Indiana Jones.

Top cop

In 1985, *Police Story* took Hong Kong action films to a new level. The fighting and stunts include a car chase down a hillside and through a village. The cars crush **tin shacks** and the chase continues on foot.

Some martial arts films, such as *Crouching Tiger*, use special effects. Jackie avoids this if he can.

Making his mark

Jackie noticed the new Hong Kong buildings had a lot of glass in them, which he wanted to use in this film. The final scene takes place in a shopping centre. Windows shatter and glass flies everywhere as the **villains** are captured.

Award winner

The film was a smash hit – everything got smashed! It won Best Picture at the Hong Kong film awards. Jackie was **nominated** for Best Actor and Best Director.

Brave co-stars

In *Police Story 3*, co-star Michelle Yeoh rides a motorbike up a ramp and jumps on to a moving train. She wanted to prove that she could do it. The practice stuntman broke his leg while testing it!

Michelle Yeoh is Jackie's co-star in *Police Story 3*.

Star words   **conquer** take on and win, or be successful
featuring including

Traffic cop

Jackie has now made a series of five successful *Police Story* films **featuring** him as a policeman. One scene in *Police Story 2* was filmed on a road in Hong Kong. Jackie was dodging real cars as well as cars driven by **stuntmen**! One stunt driver accidentally pushed Jackie along the road. Luckily, he did not fall under the car.

Goodbye brothers

Jackie made *Dragons Forever* with Samo Hung and Yuen Biao in 1987. It was the last film the three friends made together. They decided to go their own ways afterwards. Jackie still wanted to **conquer** the United States.

It's a miracle

Although *Police Story* is his favourite action movie, Jackie's 1989 film *Miracles: Mr Canton and Lady Rose* is his favourite of all the films he has made. That is because he likes the filming style and the storyline.

Jackie and co-stars at the 2004 premiere of *New Police Story*.

nominated chosen as one of the people who might win an award
tin shack hut made of tin, used as a house

31

Star quality

On song

As part of his Chinese opera training, Jackie learnt to sing. He has made 20 pop albums since 1984 and has sung in English, Cantonese, Mandarin, Japanese, and even Taiwanese. He first sang "Kung Fu Fighting Man" on the **soundtrack** of *The Young Master*.

★ ★ ★ ★ ★ ★ ★ ★ ★

Jackie is multi-talented – he sings, too!

Jackie has worked very hard to get where he is today. He is often in different places around the world, making lots of new films each year.

Getting the girl

He has managed to find some time for romance, though. He met Lin Feng-jiao at a party. She was one of Taiwan's most famous actresses. She asked him to teach her **kung fu** and he agreed. He even took his whole stunt team and equipment to Taiwan to help her on one of her films.

" When I put my mind to it, I feel I can do just about anything. "

Family fortunes

Jackie and Lin Feng-jiao got married in Los Angeles in 1983. Soon after, they had a son called Jackson Chan Cho-Ming. He is known as Jaycee.

One last try

Jackie decided to try Hollywood one more time. He knew that if he made a film Jackie Chan-style, not how US directors wanted it, it would work.

New York, New York?

In 1994, Jackie made *Rumble in the Bronx*. He thought it would be too dangerous to film in the tough Bronx area of New York.

Star words   achieve make something happen
film crew all the people needed to make a film

Instead, the **film crew** went to Vancouver in Canada. It was difficult to make the city look like New York. You can even see mountains in the background and there are none in New York City!

Conquering the United States

After becoming the top-selling film in Hong Kong in 1995, *Rumble in the Bronx* made millions of dollars in the United States in 1996. Jackie had finally made it in Hollywood!

Jackie in *Rumble in the Bronx*.

Film cast

Jackie broke his ankle jumping on to a hovercraft in *Rumble in the Bronx*. He carried on filming with his leg in plaster! He put a sock on his foot and painted it to look like he was wearing a shoe!

Jackie finally **achieved** his dream of a gala opening night with *Rumble in the Bronx*.

Awards

Jackie has been given dozens of awards during his career. As well as acting and **kung fu** titles, he received an **MBE** in 1989. He was even made an **honorary** professor at Hong Kong Polytechnic University, for services to Hong Kong tourism!

Global star

Around the world, more and more people were watching Jackie Chan films. Even though he was only just becoming known in the United States, he was awarded the 1995 MTV Lifetime Achievement Award. It was given to him for his success over so many years in Hong Kong.

Set in stone

Early in 1997, Jackie was able to **achieve** a lifelong dream. He was invited to leave his mark in Hollywood, outside Mann's Chinese Theater. His hand, foot, and famous nose print are now in concrete outside, along with his signature. In 2002, he also received a star on the Hollywood Walk of Fame, a great honour.

Better and better

In 1994, *Drunken Master 2* broke records at the Hong Kong **box office** as Jackie made the sequel to one of his best-loved films. It later did well in the United States, too.

> Jackie has been given more than one "golden popcorn trophy" at the MTV movie awards.

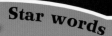

Star words

conserving looking after
honorary given as an honour

Crash, bang, wallop

Jackie then played a racing driver in *Thunderbolt*, something he had always wanted to do. The smashed cars in the film cost US$2 million! Luckily, it broke the Hong Kong box office record on its first day.

Special guest

Jackie even made an appearance in *An Alan Smithee Film: Burn, Hollywood, Burn*, just so he could star with his friend Sylvester Stallone. By the time he made *Who Am I?*, in 1999, Jackie was flying high.

★ ★ ★ ★ ★ ★ ★ ★ ★ ★

Protecting the rainforests

Jackie makes an important point about **conserving** the environment with the jungle scenes in *Who Am I?* In real life, Jackie does a lot of charity work to promote this through the Active Conservation Awareness Program.

★ ★ ★ ★ ★ ★ ★ ★ ★ ★

Jackie's star on the Walk of Fame showed that he was now a truly global star.

East meets West

The film that took Jackie's worldwide **superstardom** to a new level was *Rush Hour*. Jackie plays Hong Kong's Detective Lee alongside Chris Tucker as LA's Detective Carter. The two detectives pair up as Lee chases a gang from China to the United States. The FBI does not want their help – so they go off together and end up solving the case.

A winning combination

Now Jackie was making films in the United States in his style. He had also improved his English, which helped for Western audiences. In *Rush Hour* the combination of Jackie's physical ability and Tucker's humour worked really well. The pair have since made *Rush Hour 2*.

John Woo

John Woo (above) directed Jackie in *Hand of Death* in 1976, when they were both starting out. He helped make Jackie's film style popular in Hollywood in the 1990s. Now he is a famous director, and Jackie's friend.

Star fact

Jackie's favourite number is 32. In *Rush Hour 2*, the number on the gangster's car registration plate is 32.

Things do not always go to plan for the two detectives in *Rush Hour*.

Star words   superstardom   being a world-famous star

Shanghai showdown

After the success of *Rush Hour*, Jackie teamed up with Owen Wilson on *Shanghai Noon* in 2000. It is set in 1881 in the Wild West, and mixes cowboy adventure with Chinese **martial arts**.

Saving the princess

At first Jackie's character, Chon Wang, and Wilson's cowboy, Roy O'Bannon, do not get on, but they end up helping each other. They rescue the beautiful Princess Pei Pei (played by Lucy Liu) from her kidnappers, with plenty of adventures along the way.

London calling

In the sequel, *Shanghai Knights*, the setting moves to London. The final fight scene is set inside Big Ben. Jackie and Owen jump off the clock hand, catching hold of a flag to slow down their fall!

Sharp moves

Two real **tomahawks** are thrown at Jackie's head in *Shanghai Noon*. The **stuntmen** worked out the rhythm of the fight. Then they weighted the handles to make them fly straight. Jackie dodged, and the blades stuck in the trees they hit!

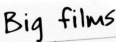

Big films

Jackie's biggest US films:
1. Rush Hour 2
2. Rush Hour
3. The Tuxedo
4. Shanghai Noon
5. Shanghai Knights

Jackie and Owen dangling from Big Ben in *Shanghai Knights*.

tomahawk type of axe

Fame and fortune

Jackie has made some famous friends in Hollywood. For a while, he owned part of the Planet Hollywood restaurant chain with Sylvester Stallone and Bruce Willis.

He always wanted to make a film with Arnold Schwarzenegger, which he managed to do in the 2004 film *Around the World in 80 Days*, where he shares a bath with him!

Family man

As Jackie gets older, he has to plan his action scenes more carefully. The films he makes in Hollywood are family-friendly comedies, with a lighter style than in the past. He now wants to be known as a serious actor, not just an action star.

World traveller

Jackie spends his time in different places around the world. Because he makes a lot of films in the United States, he spends about 3 months a year living in a hotel (above) in Los Angeles, near Hollywood.

Jackie and Sylvester Stallone are good friends!

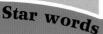
Star words   dub   change the sound of a film into a different language

Jackie's motor racing team has helped to raise lots of money for charity.

No slowing down

Jackie is still more famous in Asia than in the West. He prefers making films in Hong Kong because decisions are made very quickly and he can get on with filming. His Chinese films have much more action than the Hollywood films. Jackie thinks that everyone talks too much in the United States.

★ Star fact

Jackie usually **dubs** his own voice for the English release of his Chinese films.

Fans' favourite

Jackie loves his fans and never wants to disappoint them. He will not play **villains**, because his fans want him to be the funny good guy.

Business class

As well as being an actor and singer, Jackie is a businessman. Jackie co-owns a Chinese version of Planet Hollywood, called Star East, with lots of other celebrities, including Alan Tam, Jackie's co-star in *Armour of God*.

Car crazy

Jackie organizes an annual charity motor race. The drivers are celebrities, and it helps to raise money for a variety of Hong Kong charities. In 2004, a crowd of 30,000 people went to watch, many of them just to see Jackie.

Father and son

In 2004, Jackie appeared in *The Huadu Chronicles: Blade of the Rose* with his son, Jaycee. It was Jaycee's first film role. Jaycee is also a musician and released his first album in 2004.

Jackie co-starred with Steve Coogan in *Around the World in 80 Days*.

The Jackie Chan brand

Jackie has another range of restaurants in Asia, called Jackie's Kitchen. He also owns a Jackie Chan clothing range, with everything from jeans to suits and shoes.

Films first

Although he has made it in business, Jackie is still an actor first. On top of the *Rush Hour* series and his westerns with Owen Wilson, he made *Gorgeous* in 1999 and *The Accidental Spy* in 2001. In this film, he even fights while completely naked!

A class act

After *The Tuxedo* and *The Medallion*, Jackie played Passepartout in the 2004 remake of *Around the World in 80 Days*. In the original story Passepartout is a **minor character**, but the new version was re-written to give Jackie a lead role.

Star words   archaeologist person who studies ancient remains to find out about the past

Jackie poses next to a picture of his cartoon character.

Cartoon character

Jackie is so popular a cartoon series has been made with his name. In *The Jackie Chan Adventures*, his character is an acrobatic **archaeologist** with great **martial arts** skills. He is a secret agent, too, working for his friend Captain Black to stop his enemy, Valmont.

Computer controlled

Jackie is the star of a computer game, too. Based on the cartoon, Jackie battles against Valmont's gang, the Dark Hand. He travels around the world with his 11-year-old niece and apprentice, Jade, to protect people from ancient Chinese demons.

> I've always tried to live my life without regrets.

Family secrets

Jackie found out from his dad that he has two half-brothers and two half-sisters. He told the story of his family in the 2002 documentary *Traces of a Dragon: Jackie Chan and his Lost Family*. His real surname is Fang, not Chan!

minor character not the main character in a story

Big responsibility

In 2004, Jackie was named Goodwill Ambassador for the United Nations Children's Fund (UNICEF). UNICEF give this role to stars who have helped children. He is working with them to help stop the spread of HIV and AIDS.

Charity work

Jackie loves his fans, and he likes to give something back. He spends around half of his time doing charity work. He has even set up the Jackie Chan Charitable foundation. It helps poor children, the elderly, and the disabled.

> I always think I am so lucky. So now it's time to give back.

Helping new actors

Jackie's charity also sponsors children who want to become performers. Many of them go to the Hong Kong School for Performing Arts. It is a very different experience from the China Drama **Academy.**

Lighting the way

Jackie carried the Olympic torch on its way to the 2004 Olympics in Greece. He ran 400 metres (437 yards) with it through the Greek city of Salonika.

Jackie lights the way with the Olympic torch in 2004.

★ Star fact

Jackie's favourite film is *The Sound of Music* because it is a happy, family film.

42

Jackie has written a book about his life called *I am Jackie Chan*.

Father and son

Jackie has been busy working on his next film, *The Myth*. Jaycee has written the film's **soundtrack**.

Being the best

Jackie has gone from being a small boy, forced to practise 19 hours a day at the China Drama Academy, to a global megastar. He has always spent his life working and training hard to make himself a success. In fact, he has spent so much time working, he says he has missed out on spending time with his family and friends.

Keep on smiling

Jackie Chan has armies of fans. He has a **reputation** as one of the most daring actors and **stuntmen** in the world. What makes Jackie **unique** is the fact that he has done it all with thumbs up and a grin on his face.

A cleaner character

Even though he is rich and famous, Jackie still sweeps up at the office sometimes. This comes from his training at the opera academy where he had to keep the floors clean.

Find out more

Books to read

I Am Jackie Chan: My Life in Action, Jackie Chan with Jeff Yang (Pan, 1999)

100% Jackie Chan: the Essential Companion, Richard Cooper and Mike Leeder (Titan Books, 2002)

JC World: The Official Book of the Jackie Chan UK Fan Club, Richard Cooper (Almond Grove, 2002)

Filmography

The Myth (2005)
Rush Hour 3 (2005)
Huadu Chronicles: The Blade Of The Rose (2004)
Time Breaker (2004)
New Police Story (2004)
Around The World In 80 Days (2004)
Enter The Phoenix (2004)
The Medallion (2003)
The Twins Effect (2003)
Shanghai Knights (2003)
The Tuxedo (2002)
Rush Hour 2 (2001)
The Accidental Spy (2001)
Shanghai Noon (2000)
Gen-X Cops (1999)
Jackie Chan: My Stunts (video, as himself) (1999)
The King Of Comedy (1999)
Gorgeous (1999)
Hong Kong Face-Off (1998)
The Path Of The Dragon (video, as himself) (1998)
Jackie Chan: My Story (video, as himself) (1998)
Rush Hour (1998)
Who Am I? (1998)
The Art Of Influence (TV, as himself) (1997)
An Alan Smithee Film: Burn, Hollywood, Burn (1997)
Mr Nice Guy (1997)
First Strike (1996)
Rumble In The Bronx (1996)
Thunderbolt (1995)
Drunken Master 2 (1994)
Police Story 4: Once A Cop (1993)
Crime Story (1993)
City Hunter (1993)
Police Story 3: Supercop (1992)
Twin Dragons (1991)
Armour Of God 2: Operation Condor (1990)
Island Of Fire (1990)
Miracles: Mr Canton and Lady Rose (1989)
Black Dragon (1989)
Police Story 2 (1988)
Project A Part 2 (1987)
Dragons Forever (1987)
Armour Of God (1986)
Naughty Boys (1986)
Twinkle Twinkle Lucky Stars (1985)
Police Story (1985)
Pom Pom (1985)
Heart Of The Dragon (1985)
To Catch A Ninja (1985)
The Protector (1985)
My Lucky Stars (1985)

Wheels On Meals (1984)
Dragon Attack (1984)
Cannonball Run 2 (1984)
Project A (1984)
Fearless Hyena Part 2 (1983)
Winners and Sinners (1983)
5 Lucky Stars (1983)
Two In A Black Belt (1982)
Dragon Lord (1982)
Ninja Wars (1982)
Marvellous Fists (1982)
The Cannonball Run (1981)
The Big Brawl (1980)
The Young Master (1980)
Fearless Hyena (1979)
Dragon Fist (1978)
Magnificent Bodyguards (1978)
Spiritual Kung Fu (1978)
Snake And Crane Arts Of Shaolin (1978)
Snake In The Eagle's Shadow (1978)
Drunken Master (1978)
Half A Loaf Of Kung Fu (1978)
Fist Of Death (1977)
To Kill With Intrigue (1977)
Killer Meteors (1977)
Shaolin Wooden Men (1976)
New Fist Of Fury (1976)
All In The Family (1975)
No End Of Surprises (1975)
Hand Of Death (1975)
The Golden Lotus (1974)
Rumble In Hong Kong (1974)
Supermen Against The Orient (1974)
Eagle Shadow Fist (1973)
Attack Of The Kung Fu Girls (1973)
The Young Tiger (1973)
Enter The Dragon (1973)
Hapkido (1972)

Brutal Boxer (1972)
Fist Of Unicorn (1972)
Fist Of Fury (1971)
The Little Tiger of Canton (1971)
Kung Fu Girl (1971)
A Touch Of Zen (1968)
Big Drunk Hero (1966)
The Story Of Qui Glin (1964)
The Love Eternal (1963)
Big And Little Wong Tin Bar (1962)

Websites

To find out more about Jackie Chan, his films, and his music, try these websites:

www.jackiechan.com
www.jackiechanmusic.com
www.jackiechanmovie.com

Disclaimer

All the Internet addresses (URLs) given in this book were valid at the time of going to press. However, due to the dynamic nature of the Internet, some addresses may have changed, or sites may have ceased to exist since publication. While the author and publishers regret any inconvenience this may cause readers, no responsibility for any such changes can be accepted by either the author or the publishers.

Glossary

academy type of school

achieve make something happen

admired liked a lot

ambassador someone who works for their country, inside a foreign country

archaeologist person who studies ancient remains to find out about the past

body double person who looks like an actor in a film and replaces them in some scenes

box office place where tickets are sold. If a film does well at the box office it means that lots of people paid to go and see it.

brain oedema swelling of the brain

choreograph plan the moves carefully, like a dance

conquer take on and win, or be successful

conserving looking after

creative showing imagination

daredevil risky and brave

discipline strict rules to encourage good behaviour

dub change the sound of a film into a different language

embassy home and offices of an ambassador in a foreign country

featuring including

film crew all the people needed to make a film

flexibility bending and stretching

flop film that people do not like, and that does not make any money

fortunate lucky

honorary given as an honour

icon someone who represents something and who lots of people admire

insurance money paid out in case of an accident or injury

kung fu very old Chinese style of fighting that does not use weapons

loaned given to someone else for a short time

martial arts type of fighting based on self-defence and single combat

MBE Member of the Order of the British Empire

mime acting without speaking

minor character not the main character in a story

nominated chosen as one of the people who might win an award

out-takes scenes that were not used in a film because they went wrong

perfectionist someone who tries hard to get things right

performance acting out a show

professional being paid to do something as a job

realistic like real life

reputation being well-known for something

slapstick using actions to be funny, instead of words

soundtrack music for a film

stuntman person who stands in for an actor during dangerous scenes

superstardom being a world-famous star

super-stunt very difficult and dangerous stunt

surgeon special doctor who does operations

tin shack hut made of tin, used as a house

tomahawk type of axe

tragic very sad

unique only one

villain character who is bad

Index

Titles in the *Star File* series include:

Johnny Depp

Jane Bingham

Hardback   1 844 43283 1

Beyoncé Knowles

Mark Stewart

Hardback   1 844 43296 3

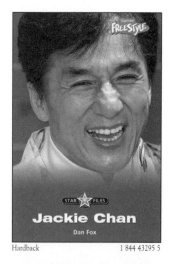

Jackie Chan

Dan Fox

Hardback   1 844 43295 5

Usher

Dan Whitcombe

Hardback   1 844 43298 X

David Beckham

Paul Harrison

Hardback   1 844 43297 1

Andre Benjamin

Brian Fitzgerald

Hardback   1 844 43972 0

Mary-Kate and Ashley Olsen

Stephanie Fitzgerald

Hardback   1 410 91662 6

Orlando Bloom

Kay Barnham

Hardback   1 844 43284 X

Find out about other titles in this series on our website www.raintreepublishers.co.uk